HOWTO ABANDON SHIP

Also by Sasha West

Failure and I Bury the Body

HOW TO ABANDON SHIP

Sasha West

Four Way Books
Tribeca

for the mother who made me daughter
for the child who made me mother

Names: West, Sasha, author.
Title: How to abandon ship / Sasha West.
Description: New York : Four Way Books, 2024.
Identifiers: LCCN 2023031692 (print) | LCCN 2023031693 (ebook) | ISBN
9781954245921 (trade paperback) | ISBN 9781954245938 (ebook)
Subjects: LCGFT: Poetry.
Classification: LCC PS3623.E8466 H69 2024 (print) | LCC PS3623.E8466
(ebook) | DDC 811/.6--dc23/eng/20230720
LC record available at https://lccn.loc.gov/2023031692
LC ebook record available at https://lccn.loc.gov/2023031693

This book is manufactured in the United States of America and printed on
acid-free paper.

Four Way Books is a not-for-profit literary press. We are grateful for the assistance
we receive from individual donors, public arts agencies, and private foundations
including the New York State Council on the Arts, a state agency.

PROUD MEMBER

[clmp]

We are a proud member of the Community of Literary Magazines and Presses.

CONTENTS

:—:

IN THOSE YEARS

And then the Berlin Wall fell and 800,000 died by machete at
the hands of the radios in Rwanda and the towers fell

swine flu and the unpaid mortgages

And when I looked up, different birds were in our trees, dogs needed
footwear in the desert not to burn their paws   We had replaced

our air conditioner and windows so our house could weather

the heat   Everything went forward   You couldn't scroll weather reports back
a day, much less a year

while our friends poured out words, everywhere, glimpses we were
trained to attend to   We kept

fewer photographs in the house, no albums   Software reminded us
to have memories   More

tragedies on the news, stronger hurricanes

We kept it at bay while we cut up garlic and tomatoes   We read to
each other on the couch   *this isn't a bad place; / why not*

pretend / we wished for it?   In one landscape, we watched the empty
pool gather tumbleweeds at the deep end

in another, clusters of people huddled on a roof   We walked
our neighborhood

The humid summer mornings released the smell of animals
voiding their bladders

and bowels in the streets   Journalists died in other countries   We
watched a man jump up and down to burst the bubble

of methane in Siberia like it was a waterbed, a joke
on someone's feed

Seneca said   *every great and overpowering grief must take away*
the capacity to choose words

since it often stifles the voice itself   Ahead were years of tundra fires
and learning

again to value kindness   Ahead the floating hospitals
and no more supply chains   The heat

dilated   We moved ourselves sideways room by room into
another home, replaced plank by plank

our understanding   On the news the countries pledged to change

slowly, so slowly   We had never before asked us
to be other than

what we were: rapacious   Where we looked the billboards

said Heaven is in goods and strippers   Buy the right bed, the right
beer, the right bed

Enter heaven through the needle's eye   Journalists were gunned
down in our country while someone sharpened

a chainsaw tooth by tooth   Looking up from
my life was a kind of vertigo   Another

body *ordered removed* by the state   And online, we
carried on   When

the seasons didn't change, our parents' neighbors photoshopped fall
foliage   Algorithms held

my gaze   Enough furry bodies to keep us
clicking   What we am I

inside of   Which of us could say when

our ship became not itself   Which plank   Which storm   We knew
we had already been silent

too long   Our shut mouths ache
Our jaws

:—:

looking at the earth, the wildwood
where the split began

—Adrienne Rich

CASSANDRA

In 3rd period, the teacher mispronounced Cassandra's wail, read:

The Seer Apollo made me too to see
a craft of woe, / To make mankind afraid

The text, a membrane tearing, then:

Cafeteria: Metal spoons rusting in my hands.

Field: Boys tackled each other, exploding
in the desert from the IEDs.

I touched my first lover, felt the hole
in dirt where his limbs would loosen.

An illness: I was walking on the gym floor, also ashes it would become.
Rot bloomed from our fridge: my parents smelled sharp
like their steel caskets.

In the science class video: stream waters
       sped, greying ozone air, the film
       stretched forward, trees became
       cattle became carcasses, the infrared
       burned, politicians shook

hands, did nothing,
a centrifuge, cities digging
preemptory mass graves
for summer, red clouds and sparks
falling, the river was planks
and bodies and I was
lighted into darkness.

Then, for 20 years, nothing.

I went back to sleep, tucking my
head under the wing of my body,
some god-blinded beast
waiting.

TRIAGE

people we love flew to us to toast us

maps of the coastline were drawn, erased, redrawn

for your hand I would give my hand

red bud trees & a silver surface of light that cuts the darkness

we gather our lives under a common roof

mosquitoes carry the disease back & forth across borders

an airplane over the ceremony cuts back

into the real world, we have opened and entered love

wild describes what the fire does, not what it is

another sliver of ice breaks from ice

if a come cry ascends the throat, if your body silvers me

we empty the earth

here in the long schoolroom of love

after the storm scatters its luminol, you can see what oil butchered

a joy that swallows the body whole

the border wall rises, the droughts dry, the crops burn

is this what dominion feels like?

back in the world's dull throb

so quiet you'd never noticed

bodies bent down the fields and the grasses and the wildflowers

we'd arrived in the American dream

WE'VE NOT LONG COME IN

Or was I in my marriage bed, stuffed with hay, or
was I in the field between the plants' burrs and hard globes
of dust in sun, or was I on the ice floor, or was I in a river
as I pushed you from my body. Once I brought you here
I could take the hood of *family*, once you drank from me,
the name of *mother*. Here I am, your animal. You have made
me flesh. I have made you to consume what the world is flurrying
even now to make. You have bound him and me together
in a ring of muscle and bone. Your hyphen weds our names.
Had I a larger tongue, I would have cleaned you myself.
I have disappeared inside your making and the joy
unbearable in its steadfast thrum. I had the low call
of it inside me always. It quakes, rearranges
everything. Give awe your lineaments—and I will birth it.

CASSANDRA

Then it started
again, at first a nerve's
tingle, like a strand of hair
or spider web against an
arm, then my daughter was
nursing, then a hill built of
fur—what animal? Great auk,
Moa, Tasmanian tiger?—settlers
wiped out the species to plant a flag
in, then the feeling of land hollowed
out below us, reports from dynamite
while I held her sleeping body, blasts
that freed the coal and the tin, a pulse
of miners in, down, out, their pickets, then
machines, oil rigs rushed up, left alone in the
wilderness, then hearing pipelines run the veins

of the country, the rock broken, the ground shifted,

then I watched the orange fur of the orangutan made

more orange by the fire that burned it, orange: the palm

fruits that grew from the ashes of its body, then its hand

and my infant daughter's hand clasped and unclasped my

finger, then slack, then I watched dust above Oklahoma, above

Phoenix: I was inside the scour of the storm, trying to see, say:

no metaphor for 5,000 feet of dust, then ashes, then soot at the

bottom of the ocean, coral bones starved and hidden below water:

then last static of a radio driving out of sound's circumference, then

flashes of dream catching back up to me: I was in the house on land that

once was ice, that once was under ocean, that once was Mexico: then time

pushed up to and past me: like being all day on the verge of a seizure, a stutter,

the whole body poised for a kind of unhousing: I became permeable to the world

THE TRAGEDY OF THE COMMONS

I would have taken the antidote
even if I knew it would mutate the virus,
Daughter, I would have put it in your body.

We will use. We will use up.

I spread the mica on my eyelids to shine
while the mica mines went slowly dull.

I hoarded the fruit to rot.

I was in this
a perfect representation
of my species.

FOSSIL FUELS

I make CO2 by breathing: burn raw the charcoal: raise methane from tundra and wetlands: I am become polluter of worlds: knock my heat against the trees: lick a rough tongue on glaciers: I pull the ocean inward: dis-own the landscape: shrink the animal's range: I am capricious: hold back rain too long in one farm: flood elsewhere crops and bridges: boil: my mind snuffs out winter: stirs fire: I greet the invasive species: dip acid fingers in the seas to dissolve the shells: collect bodies of livestock: husks of fracked-out towns: the saltwater-flooded deltas: I am chaos panting: if you let me grow I'll gullet ice shelves and slick into oceans: you've studied the trickster: you know how I work: I take: what you want and hold it in my belly: I give you back the world dis-figured: I am that I am: I extinct air by breathing

ISOLATIONISM

my daughter curled against my body: small bundle of sleep

or mad attempt to: my husband's hand on her back: my back:

now that I love: my country: it can break me: I knew so little of

our history: tethered to a shallow training: schoolrooms where

yellow pencils lay still: our tongues dumb slabs in our mouths:

we thought it was enough: not to be wrong: in those months

of our error: the bodies moldered: the years flickered out: I

chose training in the human: not in public records: and: here

she is fierce and furless on my arm: I awoke pinned: I awoke

unmoored: in the history of my country: my friends far away

and childless: I was here in the isolation: happiness makes: when

we crawl deep enough inside of it: when we make of it a stone to weigh our sleeping bodies down with: can I forgive

me: and: am I sleeping now?

THE LONG EMERGENCY

The government's belief in resource panic grew.
We watched them arm their imagination with
soldiers and detention centers. I collaged
disasters into a version of the future where
it rained iron across silt-filled houses. How easy
to picture you, dear one, trying to carry
our child somewhere safe, half-driven mad
by tidal surge, wreckage, your way lit by the hulls
of burning cars. To watch from the balcony
as the storms came closer. To see in the denuded
fields our future. My mind rushed to the very end
because it was, by definition, a wall: could a wall
contain my fear? My mind rushed water up
the sides of the windows, my mind stripped
sound from the forests, made us as close to wild
as we could be. Love, how to tell you, this was
constant: apocalypse a missing tooth my mind's tongue
ran to. I'd be in the car, daughter in back, radio on
a song she liked, and be answering some small
question, how a stick shift works, or what the march
had been about—and in my other self I'd be wondering
how far up our street the floods would lap, where
we could go for food when the crops failed. I laid
my shining dark thoughts onto every space like

gold leaf, shook foil, like I'd smudged our life out
on the palimpsest to write over. I'd once been
a child who made ghosts too real for friends,
had spent a life sharpening the blade of my
imagination until it could sculpt any substance,
quickly whittle back *what is* into its truest form.
With what was undoing, undone, I had made
myself a body. I tried, whispering to myself:
we will begin human history again. It quieted
no fears. The dreams nibbled at the places
in my flesh that looked like grass.

ODE TO FOSSIL FUEL

Without you, no paper in reams, no books with spines to break with use, no shirt whose blue I love against my husband's skin, eyes, no button from another country, no stitches programmed down his sides, no machine measuring my mother's heart while they cut the cancer out, no tomatoes in winter, no cheap wine, no wandering another country's streets for a few days, no drug mules, char in a child's lungs, no miles of highway, no fast enough to break a tumbleweed, no Christmas trees in desert, no rolling blackouts, no moving away from but still keeping family, no clean and running water, no toothbrushes, no antibiotics, no grandmother's face on the phone teasing my daughter, no ballet shoes, no hothouse flowers at our wedding, no train on my dress, no desire for a train on my dress, you have made us wealthy in goods and time, without you no cookbooks, no inflatable pool, no water guns, no smashing the bass at the end of a concert, no MTV, no Hollywood, no Hadron Collider, you have migrated the bees on the backs of trucks, you have made cement swimming pools, a million rubber ducks and most of the toys my daughter loves, without you no lifejackets, no mammograms, no gas masks, no napalm, no grandmother's farm in summer, no machines to replace bodies in the fields, no wind turbines on semis across the highways, we could have known who made every object in our house, no neatly cremated bodies behind the barbed wire, the buildings, no mercury rising through the city from their burned teeth, without you fewer mosquitoes, no almost instantaneous history of the world in light, no expansion to the coast, without you no mass-market guns, no 3D printers, no ultrasound of the baby's body, no landscape as a staging area for designer clothes & purses, no taking someone's acres to tunnel or poison, no carnival rides, no ice in drinks, no selling the oil & mineral rights to leave something to the next generation, without you no wonder, no photos of the war, the wedding, no piñata favors, no artificial heart, no snooze button, without you no body doused in flames for protest, no flying back to say goodbye to my grandparents, no flying for the funerals, no casinos, no poems scattered in dead hard drives, no soldiers on the ships and submarines sent to the sea, to war, no flag in the ice, no recording under the ocean of song, no birth control pill in its oyster pink box, no women on the factory floor, no flammable nightgowns, flammable water, oil slick, yellow bright wellies, train explosion, paintings that smell like horses, fish from the ocean's middle, no quick shower before work, no Madam Curie's laboratory, no man on the moon, astronauts exploding in air, no World Trade Center, no World Trade Center falling, no fires in the oil fields, no oil spill in the water, no time down to the second, no glut of information, no newspaper on my phone, no cold waiting rooms, no pieces showing what it all adds up to, here we are: an increased standard of living, fewer deaths in the factories, the mines, the fields, and now, bear down: the sixth extinction's crowning

23

:——:

a word past utterance, a grief
more deep than me.

—Anne Carson

BALLOON THERMOMETER C. 1975

The mercury pooled in the bulb

           then rose

slow climb

        scientists rendered

                the silvery change

in language careful

        to be exact

                Such a little change

mercury kept rising

        slowly, into neutrality

of tone

        I heard once

             a distress call

slowed down into

        a kind of music

The dying rabbit

        could have been a bird

                trilling: Listen—

to the stock exchange

                    run its silent numbers

over your face

          in light

DOUBT

They said:
from a tree
had come
our exile.

In my mind, death
was a forest
burned
to ground.
Carbon dug
from earth started
the blaze.
I believed
I could hold
difficult knowledge—
endure. I asked
to know
everything you
could tell me,
I swallowed the bitter

pomegranate seeds.
Not Eve—
Persephone

whose eating
keeps her
underground. Half
the year
my mind rewilds
itself deep in coal
mines, deep
in the artic
blaze. The tree looks

to be
living but *is*
mostly dead
wood—just a few
millimeters
under bark
and leaves make
what we see
as life.
          Rest
in the crucible
of anxiety. It will
destroy you. It
will transform

you.

> What I know has
died inside me
to make bone.

ENTERING CASSANDRA

The voice came through bare syntax: branching,

constant turning to gather in: I was myself

and other: what fur or feather my country

fantailed: *woe's wilderness called me until my call*

was perfect: The voice tried to cut to

the image: I had to learn to whittle, to waste

nothing and not to waste away: I'd come

to do the grief work: come from people fleeing

who thought blood sanctified, claimed dirt: In

childhood games, we were colonizer or colonized:

what good listeners we were to our country's

silence: my organs couldn't feel the radioactivity

gathering: Men laid down iron and tar to beckon

fossil fuels across the country—and they came: nothing

had changed: power told us pretty stories, gave us

petroleum baubles: I could see more clearly

the present: My voice put my body in the slipstream,

pollen rose around us: *this strange fire, this shining wind*:

I let go of my speaking so I could speak

HOW TO ABANDON SHIP

Cows calve, horses foal, goats kid, but women do not child.
Another verb separates us from the noun of it, a distance between
cells that split in my body, my body, and her wet fur on my stomach.

I spent all morning as an animal, all afternoon covering
that knowledge up with dirt and sticks. I scratched
out a hole to bury my shame in. Someday my bones

would be gnawed at by something with fur. I tasted
bitter adrenaline down my throat. I lay with him
haunch to haunch and rolled back my reason. Once our species

could cooperate, we could drop bombs, invent plastic, extract
fuels, burn and burn. Our forward-facing eyes made us
predator. We studied bodies we'd made extinct as a hobby.

How impossible we still roamed the countryside, still kept
ships with such large holds. The animals my daughter loves best
she distorts with love: bear's fur matted under an arm, skunk's head

misshapen with sleep. I watch her menagerie fray, try to rethread
the monkey's arm to its body, brush out the horse's tangle
of plastic mane. In her room, I can repair a species. When she

gets older someone will tell her how to groom the animal off
of herself. My body took calcium from my body to make her
milk, I nursed her with my bones. The verb nurse means to care

for in illness, to drink too long a single drink, to keep
a grudge too closely. Her cells and mine changed places,
I extracted my elements to feed her. What could be

wilder? I meant my body as a mother. Believe in my bones the risk
I feel. Weather the new war our culture tells us not to speak
of. But my body knows to go outside in an earthquake, to huddle

down when the wind blows. To bite. To keen. To howl.

GREAT ACCELERATION

we evolved to bird song

as the insects diminish

the skies quiet

my body feels

the gaps between the notes

a bounty and then

a barrenness

CASSANDRA

It wasn't easy to see, to say: I carried

in my body all the silences: the king laughing

while the men climbed out of my mouth

from a wooden horse's belly: the cop who

said I'd earn the hole in my door the man

would punch: No one believed me the way

no one believed the air: Still, I will tell you

from the back of my throat, the words still

singeing: All these centuries, the gods kept

churning out tragedies for us to pass

by, shrug off: As they evolved, the gods

learned to slow kills down, below the speed

of human naming: so from the inside

disintegration looks like a normal life:

The gods are cruel because they are

bored: they can buy anything: I have taken

my voice past the threshold, past

the lintel: I am speaking to you now from

inside the wildfire while it burns the hair

from my body: I don't expect you will listen

DOUBT IS OUR PRODUCT

We have recalibrated the winter. In our files,
we hoard your beautiful birds. The most effective
way to combat suffering is to frame the country
as being in perpetual summer. Have you read
stories of the preacher whose whole flock gave
away their earthly goods to prepare for apocalypse?
We would want to be the neighbors, waking
the next day with a full larder. We encourage
you to read Chicken Little *to your children.*
We have sped you up and spirited you over.
We brought you: tarmac and clouds beside
the airplane's wing. We brought you: traveling
the highway to woo your country. Look out
the window: flares on the left, windmills
on the right. Only one helps you navigate
the dark. Like good neighbors, we have hidden
our uglies underground so you can keep
your landscapes. If you stopped buying,
what self would you have to substitute? What
pattern of the day could make you? All that free
time our machines gave you. And you, spread
out in the energy grids of your mind with no food
to prepare or grow, no clothes to mend, no strangers
to tend to—what else is there for you to conquer

now? We enter the carbon of our bodies and then
we enter the age of carbon. We have evolved
together into the perfect mouth.

CASSANDRA

increasingly the raw flicker—I couldn't tell you—that I was
walking in the paper goods aisle and the boreal forest that fed it—
that the sequins over the children's bellies shimmered into
the bellies of the fish gutted open to glitter—that knowing how
the field would burn made the field shimmer—and sorrow caught
against my clothes like sandpaper—that red was sometimes so lush
at the edge of my vision, the slow carnage a poppy field—that
weathering steel has a skin of rust to keep the deeper self from
rusting—that I tried to rust my mind—that when I ate an orange I
became wholly orange, felt my teeth between the pulp's cells sink
into my own hand, its rot, the loam—that like an enemy leaving
a territory, the ocean salted so many acres—that trees died from
the bottom up, the forest a floating pool of green limbs over black
stone—that the visions started spreading—so many of us in waste
+ waves + endless flood—that my mind alongside their minds
was less alone, less singular—that everywhere I looked I was
a terrible window—that bonfires of burning tires around each
deer's corpse on the thawing tundra thawed the tundra—that fish
swam across the marble floor of the dictator's palace—that as we
got nearer and everything sped up, what flew off with centrifugal
force was a terrifying kindness—that the neighbors tended each
other's lives after the storms fiercely, herding debris, filling sand-
bags, tucking an old woman in on a couch or floor—had you seen
what, when we all pulled together, came from us, you would see

why my suffering faded—how tender our villages when the goods
receded back to good—yes, the world kept burning—I kissed my
daughter's neck behind her hair where I had marked her—
my husband and I lay down like the ones in Pompeii
to be together, forever, as stone

CASSANDRA'S DAUGHTER

Of course it was like that for you.

I was standing beside you when

you grabbed your head. My head

was where your words describing the world

went. When you gave the sights to me, like

a disease, the gorgeous lushness

of scope you saw was buried

in the data, the memorandum

of loss. I burned with

fever. Richer now in the experience

of information, what story

could I tell that would be

memorable? I am being shaped

into something new, waiting,

listening to birds give out song

before

the songs give out.

HABITABLE

How in courting, we compared childhoods:

running a finger over the nubby globe,

half red with codes:

deforested, desertified, deserted.

My family wasted water:

orange marigolds in a single line. His washed

clothes & sidewalks. In school we learned

water as a system

of arteries. In the mysteries

I read: bodies bled

out. The teacher asked us

to imagine we were the woman

in a Yemen without water:

opening her door

to the neighbor's news, gathering

clothes and goods. Goodbye house. Goodbye hill.

Being inside the sharpest pain:

trying it on again and again: my body

expanded into the world

through her door. What was

wrong leaked into me. Every year, more

tumbleweeds ready to burst against our car

with a loud crack. And his school assembly with slides.

The Before shots: a green lush happiness, pulsing—.

Only our parents could really imagine

                        us in a different childhood. Can I say we

didn't know? Or did—and

            didn't care when we had

                     her? What the body wants is deeper

than the mind.

              The world expanded

into my body. My body wanted more room

                  to fit the pain in.

A globe. A belly.

             If I look backwards, I can still find no map

for this—

        world as it spins out. Human need

       to tamp the worry down into the body. Now

when I imagine

the sharpest pain: you

are older.   You open your door.

DEAR DAUGHTER,

Appleseed / came to a place he didn't like / he covered it with apple trees
—*Lorine Niedecker*

years of long calm gave the animals
giant antlers and extravagant
plumage

split the earth into crisp
white ice and the stubble of buildings

the moon is still something that waxes, wanes
you paste fish onto butcher paper

I teach you the names of creatures
and birds so you will be able to write
elegies to them

PROXIMITY

in her chamber weaving a great cloth
doublefolded and red and she sprinkled into it
the many contests of horsetaming Trojans and bronzeclad Achaians
which for her sake they were suffering at the hands of Ares
—Homer Iliad, 3.126-29

Helen chose: No, Homer chose for Helen: red
cloth to receive men's battleblood: violence
folded neatly into the world woven, doubled
like a mirror: Homer's telling chose Helen as
war's cause from afar: I try to inhabit Helen's
mind: every fallen body named by messenger
was hers: like the president whose words
become troops: whose troops become casualties:
Lincoln owned in his letters every grief
the nation chose: No, the griefs reported: No
president wrote to the parents of every
man enslaved: Their bodies made the nation:
If the cotton was white and the plantation
owners were white and the historians were
white and the paper was white: then
the violence bleaches into its backdrop: like
the blood spilled in Helen's red cloth
that is red: What was it for her to hold

not bow or sword but needle?: to pull red
thread through the warrior's breastbone?: No
flag folded into a triangle carries all bodies
home: its spearpoint hangs on the hearths of
the grieving: a medal in public mourning: If you
are thinking: No, I hold no official rank, my choices
call no troops, then look: how thinking hides
a king in it: or how the world makes from
raw your money: No?: We enter the volta:
disaster the next normal: Close by: photos
of floods in the newspaper: Close by: refugees
in a convention center: No, we could have
called them neighbors: Klein says *the illusion*
of proximity coupled with the reality
of distance allows us to pretend
our dry feet mean safety: that there is no
long chain between my steering wheel,
clear grey smoke and the deluge: no long
chain between this plastic milk jug
the oil that made it and heat poured
over the earth: such a long way between
my shirt and the child's hands sewing:
such a long way between purchase
and poison: between steam engine

and catastrophe: surely my hands
don't scatter these bodies into the field?:
It is a great cloth we keep folding
and sprinkle into it: our bodies in the white
stripes: other bodies in the red: we have lived
in the illusion those stars were a crown: No,
the stars were pinned to arms and pickup trucks:
No, the stars were barbed wire tangling: No,
I have kept silent in my room: making things:
images of what has fallen across the earth:
the inevitable crest of a long red history: No: Like
Helen, clothing the battlefield in beauty: No: My
imagination inscribes it: No: To commemorate
means to remember together the same story:
No, stop: So we can plant our flag in yet another
country's horses, pipelines: No: So we can stake
down another man's sternum with red thread

CASSANDRA

Some days I could go quietly into the spot where
the man tended the boy's wounds and fed him
torn meat pulled from the pheasant's body Some days
I went into only that spot Some days only landing
in that Some days I could choose to go quickly to
the day when kindness turned the tide disaster
turned the man fed the boy by hand torn meat
from the pheasant's roasted breast Some days
almost everyone was gone their camp lingered
in front of me I was suspicious of the new world
the new world was always formed from killing
the old their scent lingered how tender Some days
I could choose just that one day boy gathered
to a stranger's body boy like pictà under the man's
face turned down I had held my daughter like that
even after she got too big the boy gathered to him by
the fire the man's hand tearing a bird for the boy's warmth
Some days I chose the boy gathered to the man's coat
fed pheasant by hand from the man's mouth from
the fire Some days I could choose The man's hand
tearing flesh The boy's mouth opening to take it

A FORGERY OF HISTORY

Shake off   that narrative   of the world.

Enough.   Just enough.   Keep

that part.   Zoom in   and   blur.

Then make   the book   about disaster

your religious text.   All it does   is name

the fires.   Drill your way through

the ocean   the factories   the graves.

Reward yourself   with a slick   drink

of oil.   I'm not telling   you

anything   you don't already know.

The voices below   your window   shout:

Neither here, nor   elsewhere. *Pretend   we are*

honest and trustworthy.   After all, you are

going to leave   your child   with us. We

will rock her to sleep   in the shale.

Already we are   whispering   in her ear

our long tale   of ever-increasing   growth.

CASSANDRA'S HUSBAND

Remember:
we marked her years
with a stick to the back
of a paper beast

Sugared wrappers fell around her feet

Rust-red cycle:
people beat the donkey's
tissue paper for candy,
the worker in the factory
spills their labor

How can we prepare
her? Blood flows to the same
part of the brain when she
remembers, when she imagines

People will arrive:
skin infected by the constant salt
water, dust in their teeth
and farms, weak and released
too early from
the pandemic hospital

And if she helps, she
can never stop knowing

we let this happen

And if she doesn't, that will
be a kind of death in her
no word will repair

How can we prepare her?

When the piñata
stops rolling in the tree,
she will be left
with the shreds
of our country

RECOGNITION

How many storms out of season—A river
rerouted, a current of goods, swelling—But trying
to act normal, all around, people in a kind of

normalcy. Storms made better footage than a slow
starvation. That summer, subway tile everywhere,
and chevrons. People dressed well, read well, ate

farm-to-table meals on one staged set or another—A kind
of illness this swaddled edge of miniature wealth, an illness
not to enjoy this playacting—I kept my mind away

from others the way a sick person doesn't
shake hands, the TV showed us what we couldn't
afford, then stores knocked down workers until

we could, and we had private traumas, deaths
and assault, brutality and sirens, enough to keep us
blindered, muddling, in sorrow, enough

not to look too closely—We had two cars, a fridge,
a washing machine, were told we were what the whole
world wanted—have you tried the cold brew coffee?

the activated charcoal cocktail? We had children
who seared joy into us—and toil—and wrote dead
letters to the government, made signs, marched

against the violences we could see—All of it filled
time the way a life does, expanded if we gave it
space, where would those future bodies

go? Where could be quiet enough to imagine
our children's limbs, neighbor's houses
in wind we'd never seen? What deserted mall

could be big enough to house the imagined
carcasses of the dying-off animals? Guilt obscures
grief, consolation burns from the inside. I tried to

enlarge my mind the way I'd eaten my pregnant
belly into expansion, swallowing each day more
facts and still I could not contain the entire

ice shelf, the size overwhelmed, the numbers
overwhelmed, at least I could put my body in a storm
to be dwarfed—my heart gulped up the graph lines,

the exponential increase. I put the two boys drowned
in mud inside my daughter's body, then the refugees
in tents, the accumulating genocide, growing speed until

none of them seemed real, until even she disappeared
when I left the room, every time I arrived at the edge
of what the human mind can do, I went back and forth

across the threshold where humans became data, trying
to keep more bodies living in the numbers, but
the disintegration spread, I could feel humans

extending as far back as my imagination could go, but
blurred and flickering forward—and I had made her
to come here and stand in the middle of what

our species had made. Who were the Greek kings
who put their daughters out to be sacrificed? I had
brought her out of my body, had her umbilical cord

cut to bind her to the rock, the mast, the world.

CASSANDRA

A kind of   Shriek   A kind   Of preaching   Whenever I opened

My mouth   Everyone thought   They   Knew   What I was

Going to say   So well   They'd never   Had to   Listen   I was

Buzz kill   Harpy   Shrill & strident   My fear was not   The fear

They'd chosen   To invest in   A moat   Larders   A catapult

Their fear   Was honey, money   With a man   Attached

Who told them   What they'd wanted   All along   That we

Deserved   That time   When   We had been isolated   And golden

CASSANDRA

You who came before us: Your generations

could look back, celebrate, mock, superior

in understanding to your ancestors, superior

in your ownership of goods: You dug

the deeper quarry, built higher, stripped more

trees bare, ignored those holier-than-thou,

brake-squealing voices: You killed, ensuring

your next kin's blood spilled, your arms could

take up arms, more war concords could

be written: You wrapped your mind onto

the world, wrapped being around you, you

were that you were, a burning bush that could not

be consumed, your mind a cloud of locusts moving

across the fields: I was there and am here and am out

where we thin to zero: I am your daughter:

I was waiting for you to make me

a landfill for history: You began to plot

how our blood would spill when you kneeled

before that portable climate

THE LOGIC OF GROWTH

*

Across the convention center floor: beds,
        sheets stretched between grey
                rails to make a room, room
                        after room, stretching across
industrial carpeting, a whole city. Woman
        curled on a cot in a house dress, man
                quieting his sons with
                        a story, the girl who leaned
into my lap until she was on it, unsure
        where her mother was in the flooded city
                the buses forced them from. Was
                        it 2005? Was it 2017? The same
convention center, the same water rising.
        My tentative arm around the girl,
                I had nothing to give her, she didn't
                        want my pity, I didn't want
my pity, I had no words for her, I taught
        her to draw a horse, breaking
                it into shapes, the torso one
                        long, squared oval, legs
akimbo. Her horse bent its neck to grass,

she had never touched a horse's head,
       she told me you blew into the nostrils
           softly, softly to calm them.

*

Daughter, you came to in a culture
with just one metaphor. The god sacrificed
his only son. The kings sacrificed daughters

to dragons or a neighboring enemy's bed. Citizens
sacrificed brothers and offspring for the wars, their
land to the toxins for the profits. And we celebrated

with flags, rifles. We taught
each new generation what glory it was
to give your child to the nation's mind.

Breath quickens and flickers. Pregnancy
took my body down to the studs, mass
shootings rang out like a nail gun.

The storms on the screen spin their scythes.
What kind of selfishness calls a body to itself
in carnage? Your legs learn to canter and rear.

My pleasure in you is worn down by the future
or does my pleasure in you wear down the future?
All the draft horses were birthed to carry coal.

*

If your country drinks down sacrifice, it
can dissolve bodies with sugar for tea, coffee, can
surrender landscape and lungs for coal,
can sell girls to the men with golden
parachutes, throw women over the rails
into the sea to make them goods, shoot
down the man in the field to water the rice,
the cotton with blood—and then around
the bones it can grow a shimmer, sugar that
sifts down a snow globe's snow, the iridescent
peacock sheen on the parking lot oil.
Daughter, you came to, new, on the back
of the Bakken fields, the Permian
Basin, your throat was worth
less than a man's, you'll dig your whole
life and never get down past the full
account of our country's plunder.

*

Heart that grew from the blood
of my heart, born to the raft of my body:
a single gallon of blood in the human body runs
the body,
             a single gallon of oil runs the generator.
What our culture longed for,
I longed for.
                    Pregnancy hollows out
the top of the breasts, the industrial age
will hollow out the mountains,
                         jellyfish
stretch their barbed shadows
across the sea.

FROM SEA TO SHINING SEA

Dear friend // the shining sea was ice // in heat // I mourn
forests not yet made // cattle ranch or paper // grass that greened
itself with rain // insects dying // in seasons // I was here before
the city windows // blew out the walls // fell to waves // here when
the grief tipped into fear // into anger // women in boats // homes
fitted into plastic bags // their legs in salt // long enough // to rot
before the calculations // let us have // grief // tears that tingle
behind the bridge // of a nose // and quicken // like milk in a breast
can feed no one // let us stay // together in the place
that aches // the taxidermy exhibit // mammals my daughter // will
not know what she misses // all the news she will // see // what
her mind will have // to become // to bear it // even if her body
will be // safe // her heart // will not // let us be salt
to each other // salt that keeps // the bodies // whole // the wound
from healing // too soon // delays the freeze // into the kind
of unseeing // that is rage // let our grief be // salt
and weep together // salt on the table // in the ocean // our bodies
surely you too // have a hand to hold // we sweat and // tender
our flesh // let our grief be // our grief let us // gather each other
back into this // homesickness

HOW TO ABANDON SHIP

In the middle of life, I found myself in a dark wood.
Was it church bells or bullets that rang out behind me?
Inside: we ticked my daughter's height up the edge of the door.

The church bells rang bullets out behind me.
Outside: the floods ticked mud up the side of the door.
A dark wood grew inside me.

In the middle of life, I found myself in a darkened country.
We lined our border in tear gas, guns, and cages.
The data showed us how to evacuate democracy.

The church rang out the hour of lead.
The government called the fleeing an invasion, as if
whiteness were a ship that was sinking.

Did the word aberration inoculate us from the pattern?
I told my husband it was a dream, he said it was the news.
Our country's wealth was a ship sinking bodies.

In the middle of lies, I foundered in a dark wood.
It was drought not war that drove out the people.
I could feel the old sublime strip the world bare inside me.

The government refused to give the crisis its name.
Like Rumpelstiltskin, the name held all its power.
Fear unfurled like a spray of bullets.

We'd given up using goat's blood to change our storms, our fate.
Wasn't it enough to change all our lightbulbs?
The floods ticked down houses, one by one.

The church rang out the hour of lead.
Each year set more precedents for the unprecedented.
My daughter was born in our sinking ship without asking.

In the middle of life, I found myself in a dark wood.
We are the accumulated heat of all people ever.
I crawl my way back to that backwards thought:

Our smallest choices make the weather.

LONGING

All those silly things I worried at
in childhood, the being left out, teased
for the second-hand clothes, girls
around me at a party who already knew
what to do in closets, cars, not yet
having my period, whether my book
would be taken, be read, would it be
remaindered, would there be
another? and who would warm my bed?
and would he stay? if my daughter would
have all her limbs, survive, nurse, if we
could buy this house, afford insurance, if
the air conditioner was really broken
yet or just on its last legs, if my friends had
forgotten me in those years I struggled, if
I would get to do my true work, if my
students liked me. What little baubles
filled my heart. All those lovely feathers
of worry that now I long for. I would
for a day pin them in my hair and pivot
in front of the mirror, gladly, and wear
a skirt and say, to no one: *tut-tut, little*
bear, it looks like rain, tut-tut, like rain.

POLITICIANS, WE ARE NOT A MUSEUM

In the hospital, we were
a tumored body coursed through
with slick oil. We had driven past
tar sands & contaminated snow
to the pixelated, white room.
You donned your suitcoats
to deliver the news.
When we entered
we stared at the X-ray, the screen,
numbers jotted on a pad. Already,
you had let the scientists
and doctors go. Though it was our body
on the film, our organs the ultrasound mapped,
you were telling us: *it is the good fortune*
of many to live distant from
the scene of sorrow.
Let us call it god that in us
let the body be burned through
with the chemicals of grief. Imagine
we every day took ourselves there
to the difficulty—
though our body trembles, through
the tears, we drive ourselves
to the room and offer our arm

to the needle. The click
of a text arriving, the steady whirr
of news. Sometimes fire
enters us in the form
of salt water or cyclone,
sometimes a dry field with husks of corn. Let us grieve:
if our prayers are answered, the future
will be only vastly diminished. We have given
each other testimonies
of fear to read at night in dark. Some
of them in markings, some in light.
We are taking your hand.
You knew the body was asking
to be saved. First you will almost
kill it.

CASSANDRA'S GRANDDAUGHTER

Or: the neighbor and I rowed through the house window. One pierced wall a lens: red shingles from the other bank dipped into our water, river flowed across our ceiling. He kissed me. Mother, what you called diminished was my world.

Or: we hooked chains around the neighbor's felled tree, dug out roads, cleared oil-soaked hay from sand, spread bumper crops. Blackouts meant stories. In drought, we traded for grasshoppers and crickets we caught in cans.

Or: every game started with government names: looter, soldier, refugee, rich man. Our hands shaped guns and drowning.

Or: the old sublime pulsed in the clouds, rewrote landscapes. Mother taught me time in disasters. Each year written with more names.

Or: the animals kept no calendars. Surprises in their migrations, mutations. Storms broke pavement like a horse throwing us off its back.

Or: I was in the rotten boards and fallen walls a keeper, building tiny shelters for the next child, something to begin again with. I sang *feather, fur, spine, and petal.*

And: I never played the role of an auditory hallucination to name what I saw. What she needed imagination to glimpse is around me.

CASSANDRA

And if, in one version, despair sank me, I sat to chronicle the end. Goodbye, veneer.
Goodbye, singularity. The images shimmered. Sometimes a vast clarity. Some-
times a joke with a glacier as the punch line. We folded disaster into routine.
Boiled water while the school bell rang, wrote postcards to politicians
to scan for anthrax. We were bailing out the boat but the banks were
sinking. We jettisoned plastic into the ocean to mark our passage.
The country hid its casualties in cop cars, its asthmatic children
in hospitals, its run-off in the streams. My umbilical cord
around my waist, my parents had put it there, my parents
chose me for this heat rising, I chose my daughter, she
chose her daughter, a long line of women who knew
things about silence, the uncanny valley of the world.
The cords held us fast to lava flowing near. I was
stuck, couldn't be helpful to others, only could
hold my daughter's hand while the ash fell,
gather her back to my body while my mind
lapped away at me, water wearing down

82

stone, tongue soothing the fur of fevered
limbs. How strange we were to each
other at the end of a written history,
these pages will flicker out when
the power goes, these pages will
rot in the libraries where bison
roam, scratching their haunches
against the shelves, where they
lay their bodies down, too,
against these spines.
Language will lose
itself, become just
a curl of grass or
twigs, recorded,
while a vast
silence crushes
our bones
slowly
to oil.

CASSANDRA'S DAUGHTER

Mother, I watched you watch

the news, watched water flood

your childhood home, saw

you overlay Houston on Mumbai,

New Orleans on Jakarta, could rhyme

really take in the scale, the thick

time of weather? I was

impatient, you seemed too easily

broken by sight, the world

was simultaneous, there were as many

types of pain as clouds, we lived

in abstraction, distraction—

Now,

I imagine those scientists inking

a map of the world that had never yet

existed—with careful fingers—as

a joke, then a warning, then watching

our country drawn

into it storm by storm.

FOSSIL FUELS

—after Naomi Klein

I had been so long away from you, in a vein
of the rock, waiting for you to find me
in peat. As you burn through
the leaves, the trees, I make you a cape
of smog. I keen in flares.
When you extract me, I am covered
in wet, like your daughter just birthed
and slick, like the bird you saw slouch
towards you from the Gulf. What is longing
but a thing that knows no
intermission. Even when you
can walk across the Gulf on rigs
you will hold and keep me. Tell me,
say: Oil is our everything. *I, who have brought you*
these clothes on ships,
and the light at night you kiss
his eyelids by, and the barrette that holds
her hair back. Whenever you gather,
I am among you. What shape
could we say craving has? My bones
in the ground become liquid
possibility. Of course, you can stop

any time you want. When we met
I said I'd steal you the sky
and there, proof of the theft,
the theft of the sky,
is the dark scrim
your lights make
of the stars. In exchange, I have
given you the Bakken flares
a bouquet of tiny orange
buds that flicker
into a quick
petal, and
burn
out.

:—:

It is I, poured out like water among them.

—Cassandra, Aeschylus *Agamemnon*

HOW TO ABANDON SHIP

One way: stop pretending your country's *newest mass horror*
will end. Go from boat to life raft directly, as if the sea were lava.

I'm stowing her scattered plastic toys, turning off glass screens'
shimmer. *Collect rain. Don't drink ocean. If water's in short*

supply, eat only sweets from survival rations. Our cooperation
brought us here. One way: say we are homesick inside our homes,

two by two. I'll grab our ditch kit, *put on all available waterproof
clothing.* Looking back: what my father's family stole to land

me here. Looking forward: our straws form lattices in the ocean's
middle. We live long enough to benefit from the passed-down fire,

not long enough to feel in our lungs the entire accumulation
of smoke. One way: erase the *poems of force*. Stop filming epics

about the glory of power. Once we could cooperate, we made
graveyards *dip and rise like the bottom of the sea*. My daughter

wants just one more princess dress, all the princesses, to hang
in the closet. *Keep warm by huddling together*. Not too late

for other models of belonging. *Keep dry, especially your feet.* Once
we could cooperate, we could invade and scale-up killing. A pile

of bodies can become a set of stairs. One way: act calm while
the ship sinks. Let danger pulse inside your body. The oil sheen

will mark you. Your inland cities will sometimes now be islands.
Arrange for lookouts. Use red flares only when they'll be seen.

Once, we could cooperate. *Collect all available flotsam. Go a safe
distance from the sinking vessel.* One way is to light the beacon.

How long we together have protected the resources of the rulers.
Note present position. Send out MAYDAY message. Join hands

to fend off the mass-made doom-yearnings. Join hands, hold
like the iceberg's lattices that can break open the ship's metal hull.

CASSANDRA

When you imagine yourself

      into the future

as a kind of doom   remember

I have watched the whole ocean rise

      like a stuttering pulse   On that last day

when the rising stops

      I have stood   where you stand now

to look out   And the water

      is only itself   cold + grey + shifting

You never saw

      the species

      your parents mourned   When you populate

your mind

        with passenger pigeons

they are as imaginary to you as

       the creatures   in your daughter's childhood fables

You think you mourn

      what the world will be for her

No: you mourn what it will be for you

      to watch it change

CASSANDRA'S DAUGHTER

I thought you were infallible. Now

I understand the visions

came from your body, that each empire

has its own fever dreams

of destruction. Wouldn't

any conqueror fear

the dispossessed? We were burning

down the acres behind us

before the army

of trees

could come

to reclaim them.

CASSANDRA'S HUSBAND

When you stand by the sea line in the future
I am not there
our daughter is not there

that doom you went to in your mind
chose shipwreck

what is it to love someone
so sick with the future tense?
like standing on an iceberg
thawing

my feet
in the sea
feeling it pulse up
my ankles
my shins
my groin

what would happen to our daughter
would happen to both
of our bodies

as far as we could thrust them into the future

why couldn't you just love
us, in the present, take
happiness the way every human
before us had: as something
time would already
cut short

who cared why
or when or how

or why

I PRAY FOR A DIMINISHED WORLD

Bark beetles emit chemicals that call each other
to the trees, to widen the browning forest. Love,
I called you to me. You came across oil, tarmac,
and sand to this dry place. We use up its water

on our backs and lemon tree and pans. Together
we make another little mouth. Outside our well-
sealed windows: flooded furniture piled
in walls up the side of suburban streets, fires

quickening, a city's rebar shaken to raw
by fracking, the slick reflection where the ocean
runs its salt tongue over the land: Gods came
from being at the mercy of the world's

fields. In drought, people turn the empty silos
into a gun. Bargain in the world's marketplace:
can drought stop somewhere? can water stop
rising? We cannot transplant the organs

of ice sheets, oceans. We cannot grow in our lungs
the forests back tree by tree. Our lemon tree
is lopsided, thirsty, freezes easily, gives no
nourishment, is only a kind of beauty. Our daughter

brings me a lemon—thorned limb gone, waxy with
a warm yellow smell—what is there to be but happy
with a kind of burning? And my husband's lips on my
neck, and the way his hands know all my body. What

should I do with their bright beauty that forms
the bulk of my days? There is no prayer that keeps
it all, given what we have made of the air. A flaw my heart
starts with him, our child, then radiates out, that I can't

every day feel in my muscles the fur pressed
into our house behind the thermostat. God, we need
reminding, the mind lets go of the hand, the mind
lets go, and still your body wants to bargain. Let

the birds that flew through arroyos in my youth
be quiet forever. But let each of us keep our daughters,
our people, some of the species that have been
catalogued. I have preserved these lemons in salt.

They glow in our fridge with a kind of sun.
I will carry the jars as far as I can
when we flee. I am bringing you
one, stranger, for our travels.

CASSANDRA'S DAUGHTER

You had the luxury of existing

in all times at once. Now we are back

in the present. We are in the middle

of telling each other stories,

trying out various myths, various

villains to explain

what the world is

to our children.

:—:

CASSANDRA: REVISION

And then I woke. Even my hope had been warped
by those old human lies: singular redemption
self as fulcrum: But other bodies had started
the burning before me: after me other bodies would
cover the last cooling ember: We wanted an easy way
out: decision on high, coordinated war effort: Not how
an ecosystem works: the big idea plundered,
erased: My country had sold me on the future:
Its fiction filled all my thoughts: When the visions
subsided, I found we: and entered: I joined my daughter's
keen limbs, my husband's gentle mind: We put our bodies
into the narrative, our hands in dirt: Beasts got louder or
we heard their speech more delicately: We tended
our imaginations: kept rewriting the doom: We unchained
ourselves from Prometheus's stolen fire: Around us, we
learned to remember: protected crops with trees, sank
sun into salt to hold and our homes: Waited for wind,
rain: A plenty: The same hand redirects our gaze from the pain
as from the paradise: The winters were gentle: We brought
people to shelter: dulled our yearnings: cut down
barbed wire: The borders and coasts lapped into
our yards: We wore down objects with our hands'
gratitude: gave: and gave again: What machine or law

could hold us back while we worked: to rush
the world back to gathering.

STORYTELLING

We play a game called what is me:
I touch the air in front of her: *not*
me: She breathes the air in: *me*: I put
the glass in front of her: *milk*: She
drinks: *me*: She turns the tree's
lemons into herself and the dirt
in the carrot's skin: I point to
the sun in the sky: *not me*: and
to her skin where it warms: *me*:
She pulls water air soil into, out
of her body: A stranger's illness:
not me: Their virus in her: *me*:
Her body's carbon makes carbon
dioxide: *me*: from plants that clean
the air we make a meal: *me*: The story
I tell her burns her neurons: *me*: My
days go into her body and come out
night: In my womb her cells became
hers and grew: *me*: In the air they
crown and grow and compose: *not*
me: Her flesh passed through my
flesh: Her body makes mine permeable

PACT

Having told a distance of weather Having clothed
each year my body a little less Having red
birds disappear from my yard a red cough burrow
to the bottom of my lungs Having a camera
Having a climate Having my face on the screen
in your hands Having a future made of what goods
would evolve to Having dehydrated ice cream Having flight
Having praised disposable tampons or lunchboxes or tv
dinners My appetites launched a thousand shipping
containers Having watched yellow hurricanes spin
behind the newscasters Having paid more for tomatoes
more for bread Having at night the glow from
a distant fire Having a mushroom cloud in my head
as a measure of panic Having the replay button Having the replay
Having sadness I wished rid of in packages Having her
body in my arms as a kind of promise Having come
to the understanding more in sorrow than in anger
Having renounced all worldly goods Having come
to you—head bowed—begging

CASSANDRA'S GRANDDAUGHTER

CASSANDRA

Every birthday, I ask
to grow the kelp forest.

                                        I ask light to flood
                                                my vision.

Will deserts really spread? Will we live
on floating islands made of garbage? Will
jellyfish bloom outside our door?

                                        Already, so many live in tents.
                                             A state within a state.

Someone chose that.

                                        To gentle an invasion,
                                           you have to open the gate.

Will we all keep our personhood?

                                        Erase the myth insulating you
                                             from a yellow jerry can. Join
                                             people born into this work.

What I learned in school is useless.

                                        A can of oil equals eight
                                        days of a person's labor. Coal

                                                  lights a room with a rainforest.

I'm trying to understand why.

                                           We were in the business of
                                           unyoking time from time.

In school, they told us to whitewash roofs
and mountains with paint.

                                           A kind of playacting at being
                                                an ice shelf.

Someone will have to redraw all the maps.

                                           Someone will remember
                                                the other stories
                                          we could have inherited.

Was oil a kind of god? Why were people
afraid to say its name?

                                           It slicked our way across Earth
                                              then into it.

You said we weren't the protagonist.

                                           Grasshoppers chew field to tatter.
                                          We handed down what helped us kill.

The wind is quiet through turbine
blades but still the birds fall.

                                        In radiation, what can save
                                            and destroy are one.

The butcher told me it was kinder
to put one hand on the animal's neck,
one on the blade.

                                    Child, nothing welcomes our force.

My teacher said all good myths
restore the social order.

                                            Your body is an order
                                                of cells remade
                                            every seven years.

I worry what comes next.

                                    Disruption can be a kind of hinge.

Will we learn to be good stewards?

                                    Our minds descended from gutting
                                        the bird open to read
                                            our fortune.

THE END

finally our minds made   porous, when
the future dimmed   people

in formation   tenderness

the abattoirs closed   fewer planes
a vast listening

across the world   animal herds
took back migration routes   pollen rose in clouds

at the edges   a slowness in the day
in the heat   a decision to rest
like a body that finally accepts   the diagnosis

bison's fur   covering us
in the rare and colder winters

so many marching   ballots and boycotts
people laying down the arsenals   of wealth

we gave up our plumage   we set aside our giant antlers
not the chaos   government predicted

ruminants remade   grasslands
microbes engineered   the soil

I let myself   come fully back
to the present   welcome

cold against the backs   of my fingertips
walking down the road   my husband brushing hair
out of my face   with his warm palm

my daughter launching   her body against me
as hard as she could   I held her
watered and sheltered trees   I opened our windows

remembered I had   the same ending

as every human   and a body
in the meantime   to run

the world through

CASSANDRA'S GRANDDAUGHTER

In summers we work at the hatchery clearing debris, helping small coho along the water. In winters I hide dried berries for foxes, fill birdfeeders with seeds that the summer didn't take. You ate only what someone else grew. I gather insects to feed my goats. I won't say food tastes better or that I am holier than your city. Mostly I am tired of hearing about your beauties. Once upon a time, infinite choices stretched in front of you every morning. Every choice you made curtailed mine. We laugh at your ridiculous suits, heels that extended your legs. No, I'm not a purist, I have music in a box and paint my toes the iridescent blue of a peacock feather's eye. Your old stories were useful though not for what you thought. I extracted from them lessons about how to grow crops, to life-hack objects, the way one could throw out most of Odysseus's story and learn to sail a ship. When you were still alive and apt to get weepy over what you saw as rubbled landscapes, I was impatient. Only a tourist fetishizes the ground where tragedy occurred. The rest of us treat it like the cemetery in the middle of town, pointing both backwards and forwards. You who knew so much were scared of the things even my toddlers know: everything comes out of death, everything returns to soil. You wanted Victorian mourning bracelets of hair and dried flowers, electronic always-ness. It required so much burning, a treadmill that ran past no mountains, no streams. Your grief a static luxury. I remember one day on the subway when cars still ran, you shamed a woman beside us who had put the money to feed a hundred mouths on her wrist. You whispered fiercely in her ear the name of each body dangling. We don't hide those of us who struggle away from the others. I would say we are more honest, exact with language. What needs to be done, we do. We act in tiny increments.

THE UNCANNY VALLEY OF THE WORLD

In the middle of life, I found myself
in a dark wood. From such little
I had made enough: bought
a car, house, diapers, food
from other countries, food I let
spoil. I circled the tv like a god.
I shed and gained a self, quantities
of wine and meat. Each new person
I was needed different clothing.
The year I was born, my parents named
me, scientists named the crisis. The dark
knowledge and I grew our bodies. My skin
glistened with its fuel, my mind clicked,
a lighter, turning. Journalists and
museums tried to edit the story into
our attention spans, our tourism. The tv knit
and unknit people's lives each night. When
the street flooded, I watched the water
lick its way up the lawn. But then recede.
Snow became imaginary but who missed it.
I inhaled dust, I drove through the vast ash
landscape of fire, swore allegiance
to myself alone in a car and called it freedom.
I could drive my own horse into the oil slick

ground, the earthquake's echo. Nothing
in my daily life suggested I was enlisting in
a national disaster. And when the lies
peeled back, peeled off, there was my country
unvarnished—what I had called aberration
was its true mind. I was born into the luck
of strip malls and safety. I was born a part of the death
squads roaming the planet's woods. Each day
a few more trees had been cleared to make
my life. In the middle of life, I pulled my daughter
close, out of a dark wood, and my husband. I sewed us
into the hide of a lion. We couldn't see, we had claws.
We roamed the wild by smell. We might be the end
of human history. Her little arms wrap around
my leg, his hand on my waist, we move together
going deeper, rough beast into the forest.

THE SHIP OF THESEUS

The sailor planing

the wood to replace

the single plank

began

the remade ship.

The ship was static.

The ship skimmed the water.

Start again:

a blade

revising.

A single plank.

:—:

ACKNOWLEDGMENTS

Many thanks to the editors and curators of the journals, anthologies, and exhibitions in which these poems first appeared (sometimes in different versions).

Agni, American Poetry Review, Borderlands, Crazyhorse, Diode, Ecotone, Florida Review, Georgia Review, Kenyon Review Online, Laurel Review, The Missouri Review Online, Notre Dame Review, Pleiades, Plume, Poetry Northwest, The Rupture, Tribes, Tupelo Quarterly, The Long Devotion: Poets Writing Motherhood (University of Georgia), *Out of Time: Poetry from the Climate Emergency* (Valley Press, UK).

Collaborative exhibitions with artist Hollis Hammonds: *A Dark Wood Grew Inside Me* (Texas A & M Wright Gallery); *Awake in the Dark* at the Columbus College of Art and Design Beeler Gallery, Austin Public Library, the College of Mainland gallery, and *The Femme Abstract*.

The following sources and poems are in direct dialogue: the 1969 Brown and Williamson Tobacco Company memo + "Doubt Is Our Product"; Aeschylus *Agamemnon* + "Cassandra" poems; Seneca and Jorie Graham's "Over and Over Stitch" + "In Those Years"; "The Priest in the Trees" *Harper's Magazine* Dec. 2016 + "Doubt"; the last line of my first book, *Failure and I Bury the Body* + "The Long Emergency"; Dante's *Inferno* and Emily Dickinson's "[After great pain, a formal feeling comes]" + the second "How to Abandon Ship"; various online advice for abandoning ships and Masha Gessen's "Never Remember: Searching for Stalin's Gulags in Putin's Russia" *Harper's Magazine*, Feb. 2018 + the third "How to Abandon Ship"; *La Temp du Loup* (dir. Michael Haneke) + "Cassandra" ["Some Days I could go quietly"]; *Winnie the Pooh* by A. A. Milne + "Longing"; *Common Sense* by Thomas Paine + "Politicians, We Are Not a Museum." Immense gratitude to the various scientists, journalists, thinkers, and artists who formed the speakers' imaginations and their factual understanding of the world in which they find themselves.

First readers—Charlie Clark, Taffy and Martin Kim, Emily Pérez, Leslie Harrison, Tomás Q. Morín—and last readers at Four Way—Martha Rhodes, Ryan Murphy, Bridget Bell—these poems are better for your minds moving through them. Thank you.

I'm grateful for the communities that held and inspired me: Jill Meyers, Ian Varley, Emily, Nina McConigley, Tiphanie Yanique, Keya Mitra, Jericho Brown, Amanda Nowlin O'Banion, James Allen Hall, Leslie, Hallie Richmond, Jason Schneiderman, Tomás, Katy Didden, Hasanthika Sirisena, Jennifer Cheng, Maurice Manning, Kate Daniels, Brigit Pegeen Kelly, Victoria Chang, Erika Meitner, Mary Helen Specht, Tyler Stoddard Smith, Zoë Fay-Stindt, Laurie Filipelli, Carrie Fountain, Owen Egerton, Roger Reeves, Travis Helms, Cyrus Cassells, Laurie Saurborn, Lisa Olstein, ire'ne lara silva, Sheila Black, Nancy Reddy, Amanda Johnston, Dale Bulla, Jonathan Lowell, Heather Houser, Amy King, Chloe Honum, Tarfia Faizullah, Diane Seuss, Aimee Nezhukumatathil, Traci Brimhall, Ada Limón, the amazing LLL Austin crew too numerous to name, the Loma Linda fellows, the Cherrywood Poetry Workshop, and the LWA who turn words to actions. I'm equally grateful for the families who are at the heart of everything—Taffy & Martin, Doug West, Sue & John Clark, Kathe MacLaren, the Clarkleys, Andy and Deborah, and the Buitragos.

Thanks to WRIT for being an amazing department of folks and to the administration for the grants + releases that helped me pursue this project. To my colleagues and students at St. Edward's University who hold the world under such tender, hopeful scrutiny. To Hollis for opening up new trajectories of poetry. To the Bread Loaf Writers' and Environmental Conferences and the Poetry at Round Top Festival for letting me share these ideas and poems. To the indie booksellers and organizations who keep our city reading.

To C, for walking with me through darkness and being willing in every part of our lives to build a new world. To Z, for who you are and for the wonder (and wandering) you make inside each day. I love you both to the almost-end of the world and back.

ABOUT THE AUTHOR

Sasha West's first book, *Failure and I Bury the Body*, won the National Poetry Series, a Texas Institute of Letters award, and a Fellowship from the Bread Loaf Writers' Conference. Recent poems have appeared in *American Poetry Review, Ecotone, Georgia Review*, and *The Long Devotion: Poets Writing Motherhood*. Her collaborative multi-media exhibitions with artist Hollis Hammonds have been shown at Texas A & M's Wright Gallery and the Columbus College of Art Design Beeler Gallery, among others. She lives in Austin, TX, where she is an associate professor of creative writing at St. Edward's University.

WE ARE ALSO GRATEFUL TO THOSE INDIVIDUALS WHO PARTICIPATED IN OUR BUILD A BOOK PROGRAM. THEY ARE:

Anonymous (14), Robert Abrams, Michael Ansara, Kathy Aponick, Michael Anna de Armas, Jean Ball, Sally Ball, Clayre Benzadón, Adrian Blevins, Laurel Blossom, Adam Bohannon, Betsy Bonner, Patricia Bottomley, Lee Briccetti, Joel Brouwer, Susan Buttenwieser, Anthony Cappo, Paul and Brandy Carlson, Dan Clarke, Mark Conway, Elinor Cramer, Kwame Dawes, John Del Peschio, Brian Komei Dempster, Patrick Donnelly, Lynn Emanuel, Blas Falconer, Jennifer Franklin, John Gallaher, Reginald Gibbons, Rebecca Kaiser Gibson, Dorothy Tapper Goldman, Julia Guez, Naomi Guttman and Jonathan Mead, Forrest Hamer, Luke Hankins, Yona Harvey, KT Herr, Karen Hildebrand, Carlie Hoffman, Glenna Horton, Thomas and Autumn Howard, Catherine Hoyser, Elizabeth Jackson, Linda Susan Jackson, Jessica Jacobs and Nickole Brown, Lee Jenkins, Elizabeth Kanell, Nancy Kassell, Maeve Kinkead, Victoria Korth, Brett Lauer and Gretchen Scott, Howard Levy, Owen Lewis and Susan Ennis, Margaree Little, Sara London and Dean Albarelli, Tariq Luthun, Myra Malkin, Louise Mathias, Victoria McCoy, Lupe Mendez, Michael and Nancy Murphy, Kimberly Nunes, Susan Okie and Walter Weiss, Cathy McArthur Palermo, Veronica Patterson, Jill Pearlman, Marcia and Chris Pelletiere, Sam Perkins, Susan Peters and Morgan Driscoll, Maya Pindyck, Megan Pinto, Kevin Prufer, Martha Rhodes and Jean Brunel, Paula Rhodes, Louise Riemer, Peter and Jill Schireson, Rob Schlegel, Yoana Setzer, Soraya Shalforoosh, Mary Slechta, Diane Souvaine, Barbara Spark, Catherine Stearns, Jacob Strautmann, Yerra Sugarman, Arthur Sze and Carol Moldaw, Marjorie and Lew Tesser, Dorothy Thomas, Rosalynde Vas Dias, Rushi Vyas, Martha Webster and Robert Fuentes, Abby Wender and Rohan Weerasinghe, Rachel Weintraub and Allston James, and Monica Youn.